THE ULTIMATE GUIDE
1 HOUR
EMAIL MARKETING

© Alan O'Rourke
All rights reserved. No part of this book may be reproduced or transmitted in any form or by any means, electronic or mechanical, including photocopying, recording, faxing, emailing, posting online or by any information storage and retrieval system, without written permission from the Publisher.
All content and images copyright of the respective companies.
For more resources and guides visit http://audiencestack.com/static/books.html

Chapters

1. Email is Dead!..4

2. Email in your marketing mix 8

3. Getting subscribers 12

4. SPAM..17

5. Email one: Retention 21

6. Designing emails for results 26

7. How to send - ESPs..29

8. How often to send 30

9. Checklist for sending your first mail newsletter 32

10. Email two: The sales email 34

11. Anatomy of a newsletter..38

12. Landing pages...40

13. Tracking and analysis 42

14. Measuring ROI..44

15. Segmenting subscribers 46

16. Automation 50

17. Re-engaging old email lists 58

Your finished email marketing plan 63

Resources and links 65

How to use this book

What do you mean how to use this book? It's a book for figs sake.
Well yes, you are right, kinda. You see this book is based on an email marketing course I have delivered for years on a couple of different Digital Marketing Diploma courses. Thousands of companies paid a lot of money to upskill their marketing and sales teams to keep up with current digital trends. I have always been very conscious of students (and their companies) getting their money's worth and leaving with an actionable plan they could start right away. Theory can be great but it is useless if you cannot turn it into practical next steps.

With that in mind my students, and now you, get a one page worksheet to take notes with during the course and reading this book. It is designed so your notes fill in the blanks. At the end of the course you end up with your email marketing plan for the next 12 months. A plan you can start today.

Download the worksheet as a word doc or .pdf at
http://audiencestack.com/static/download-book-1houremail.html

And keep it and a pen with you while you read this book.
Enjoy.

Alan

1. Email is Dead!

"Email is dead" screamed the headlines from Fortune and Inc magazines.
Facebook killed email they said.
Then Twitter killed email.
Google Wave killed email (does anyone still remember that?)
Now Slack is the new email killer (btw I love Slack!)

And yet you still have an email address. Email is stronger than it has ever been. The problem is for years I've spent time with designers, developers and even some marketing people who would say the same thing.

"Email must be dead, because I never open emails like that."

But what you must realise is that you are not your target market, and your friends are probably not your target market. Somebody is opening those emails, and people are spending billions of dollars based on those emails.

While you, your parents and your friends may not be interested in an email mentioning Justin Bieber's concert dates and ticket prices, millions of his fans are. Email marketing works when you put the right email in front of the right people at the right time – then it becomes a highly effective marketing tool that people want to read.

Let's be honest, there's nothing glamorous or sexy about email marketing. It doesn't grab the headlines like Facebook or Twitter and you can't follow celebrities. Email is... old. But the fact it is still around means it must still work. And work it does. The beauty of email is that it is so personal and direct. This is what makes it so effective.

The fascinating thing about the email killers mentioned earlier is that they quickly turned to email to increase their user engagement and growth. The backend of social media sites all involve sending emails of every notification you receive. Instead of killing email they have actually increased its usage.

And let's not forget, without an email address you can't even start a social network account.

Facebook, Twitter and LinkedIn have all redesigned their emails to increase engagement and drive traffic back to their sites. But that shouldn't be a surprise when you read reports stating the amount of people creating email accounts is going to increase from 3.6 billion to 4.3 billion in the next year. And there's a very good reason why email works so well. That's because almost everybody has it. Of the 3.6 billion email addresses currently in the world at least half of them are checked daily.

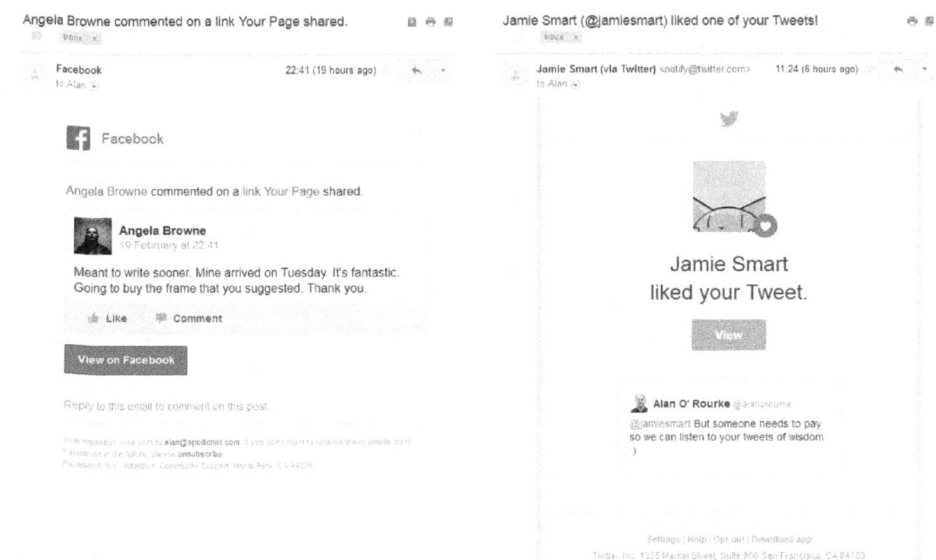

...email marketing provided the second best ROI (Return on Investment)of all online marketing methods.

Econsultancy.com, one of the leading market research sites on the web, concluded that email marketing provided the second best ROI (Return on Investment) of all online marketing methods (SEO was first).
A report from the The Direct Marketing Association of America put a value on that ROI at $38 for every $1 spent. So for every $1 you spend you could generate up to $38 compared to traditional media. For comparison, direct mail generates $25 and $15 is the return for press advertising. Another recent report put the value of a good subscriber at $128 over the lifetime of that subscriber. If you had 1000 subscribers what would that do for your business?

Successful email companies

Here are a few successful companies built on email:

You may have come across Groupon.com. It is an online company which started outemailing amazing daily deals on products and services in your local area. You purchase vouchers at great prices which are then emailed to you. At its height, Google offered to buy Groupon.com for a cool $6 billion!

HelpAReporterOut.com is a very smart concept fundamentally based around emails. A newspaper reporter has a story. She is looking for sources so she fires an email out to the database of subscribers. You as a subscriber are looking for PR opportunities. You look out for stories related to your industry and where you can help. The reporter gets an expert for her story and hopefully you get some press coverage. This is a win-win situation, or at least it was to Peter Shankman who sold his service, essentially an email list, for $8 million.

Thrillist.com started as a daily men's publication which reaches over 5 million people each day via email. It showcases the latest styles, stories and places to go. At the time of writing this the site has generated more than $40 million in sales via its email newsletter.

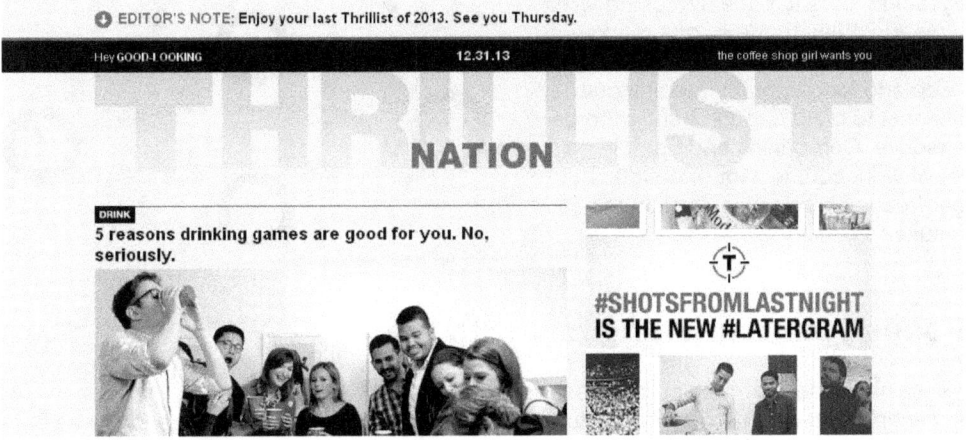

Bloomberg is a media company delivering business news from around the world. In 2011 they launched Bloomberg BRIEF. A selection of newsletters delivering the latest news, market data, and expert commentary from the world's most trusted economists and analysts. Two years after launching they reported over 230,000 paying subscribers.

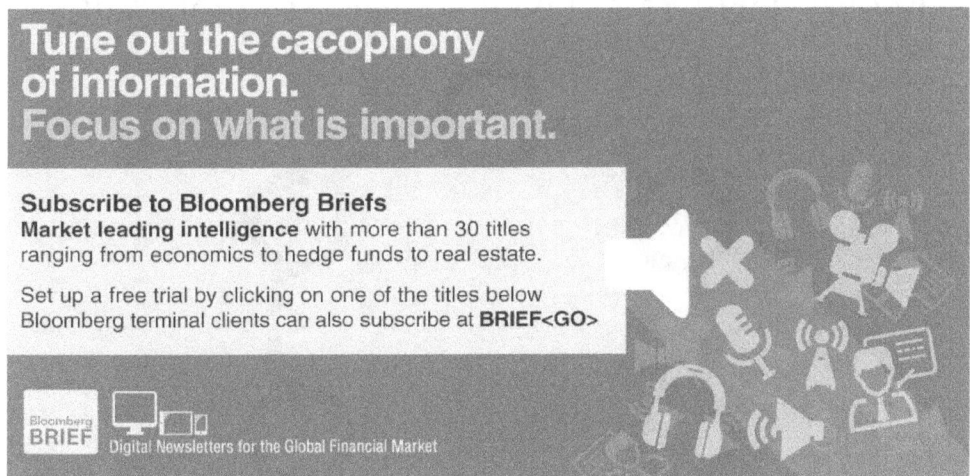

The list goes on (pun intended! Sorry, I will try not to do that again in this book!)
All signs point to email being alive and well and actively thriving. Email is most definitely not dead. So how do you make email work for you?

2. Email in your marketing mix

Let's talk about where email fits into the total marketing mix. Most people take a very scattershot approach to their marketing. They might blog from time to time. Maybe they update Twitter, LinkedIn and Facebook. They might even go offline with flyers and newspaper ads once in a while. This is like getting a shotgun, closing your eyes and firing it in the air hoping to hit a pigeon. They run from one marketing channel to the next, never really delving deep and long enough into any one channel to build enough traction to be effective. Companies end up doing a lot of work across a lot of outlets, but get frustrated because they don't see results.

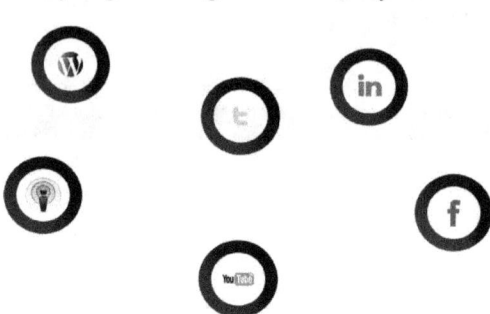

Focus your marketing mix with email.

As we have seen with the companies mentioned, you can build your value in your subscriber list. Add some strategy to your marketing approach. Promote and push your content and promotions through these various channels BUT ALWAYS pull the user back to your email list. Once a user is in your list you can start building a relationship with them until they are at a stage where they are ready to buy from you or recommend you to others.

Always pull the user back to your list

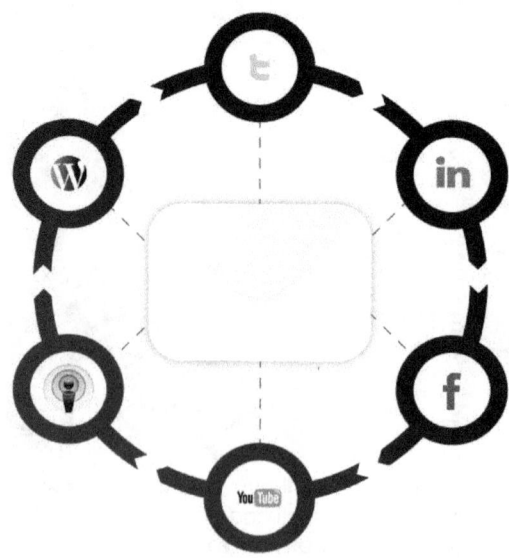

This is the way I approach my own marketing, especially for content marketing. Here is a simple breakdown.

Write once, publish EVERYWHERE and EVERYWAY.

The approach I tried is based on the premise of write once, publish EVERYWHERE and EVERYWAY. I produce one detailed, great piece of content. Preferably evergreen, i.e. the content is not time sensitive and will always be useful. Then I break up and reformat that content for release on different channels over a period of one month or longer.

Over a 30 day period I will do the following:

- Publish one piece of anchor content a month e.g. an eBook on a single topic. It can be small, about 6-7 pages. Big text and lots of pictures. But it must cover the topic well.
- Split the eBook into weekly blog posts.
- Tweet excerpts. Not just the book title but tweet quotes from the text.
- Repost the blog posts to Linkedin Pulse, groups and other forums. Put a one week delay on these to let the blog get indexed by search engines first. Post the full content. People will appreciate it and still click through to download the eBook.
- Use the content to answer questions on sites like Quora.com. If you find it hard to find people asking questions that your content answers, then you may not be writing the right content.
- Set up alerts on social media for people asking questions around the topic so you can share the content.
- Take the images from the eBook and post to Flickr under creative commons so people can use (if they link to you). This is a slow burner but works great. I have got links from Forbes, Inc, Mashable and others using this.
- Do a press release.
- Do a webinar for the content and invite people from outside your existing subscribers as well.
- Post the webinar slides on Slideshare.
- Post the video recording of the webinar on YouTube.
- Promote any of the above content with Pay Per Click ads.

EVERYTHING must end with a call to action back to your site, where you try and capture an email address and grow your audience and leads.

I break this down further with ideal times to publish on each channel here: http://audiencestack.com/static/blog-one-month-micro-b2b-marketing-plan-infographic.html

Growing your email database is going to be of real value to your business success. That database of leads—people who are interested in you, your product, your services—is where the long-term value of your business is built up. Use each channel as an invite to encourage a prospect to sign up. Use email as your core customer list. It means when you push some marketing out to YouTube or Twitter, even if half of your audience is over on Facebook or LinkedIn, you can go back to your core email list and let them all know.

When HelpAReporterOut.com was bought, the buyer was procuring the core database of an engaged audience and customer base, so they could continue selling to them and growing the business. Your email, directed to your user, is prompting instant action. You are now in charge of your communication with your user. Users are prospects, and then customers, and now, because of email, you hold that value. Facebook, for example, could suddenly start charging thousands of euros a month for a business page.

Use each channel as an invite to encourage a prospect to sign up. Use email as your core customer list.

Do you remember the social network MySpace? It was one of the most popular social networks. Rupurt Murdock's News Corp bought the site for $580 million. But then Facebook rose to dominance and stole all the thunder from MySpace which eventually died a death. If companies asked their MySpace fans for an email address they could easily have followed them over to the new network. Instead they had to start from scratch again. With a basic email address you can find a full profile of each user online, and as they move from one social network to the next, you can stick with them and you can invite them to connect on each new successful network. Now, that's where your long-term value lies.

By using tools like FullContact.com and Rapportive, you can take a person's email address and find out what social networks they are on.

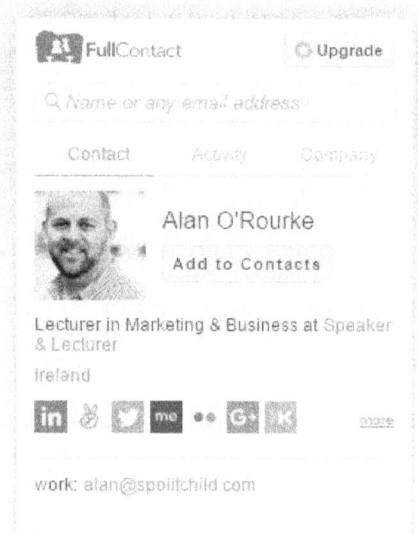

The ultimate guide to email marketing in 1 hour

Worksheet step 1

Fill out this worksheet after every section. It will build up step by step your email marketing plan so you can finish this book with practical next steps to follow.

Download the worksheet at:
http://audiencestack.com/static/download-book-1houremail.html

For the first step of the worksheet you need to decide why you are doing email marketing. Why do you or your boss want to do email marketing? Is it just because you think you should be doing it and everyone else is?
Do you want to retain and engage your existing customers?
Do you want to build an email list to sell to them?

Decide what your primary objective is and write the goal down in the worksheet. Check back on this after 3, 6 and 12 months to see if you are achieving it. If not you need to change your approach.

3. Getting subscribers

There are two key types of email newsletters.

1. **Customer retention mails.**
   These are for holding onto existing customers and audiences to remind them that you're still around. They may not need to buy from you now but when they do you will be the first they think of. I often call this the "I'm not dead" mail.

2. **Sales campaigns.**
   These are the emails you send when you want to sell a particular product or service.

But before that, we need subscribers to send an email newsletter to. Let's look at lead generation and getting subscribers.

You can't get started in email marketing until you have someone to send an email to. You need subscribers so let's look at some basic ideas for building your subscriber list.

1. **Ask.**
   In many cases, getting a subscriber is as simple as just asking. In fact, recent research has shown that asking a user of a website to subscribe to a newsletter is probably the most effective way to build a subscriber list.

   Keep your opt-in forms simple. Unless you plan on sending your subscribers Christmas presents and Easter eggs, just ask for their first name and email address at first.
   Below (left) is an example of asking for too much information. Capture the email address first, and then you can always come back and ask for more information later, if you wish.

 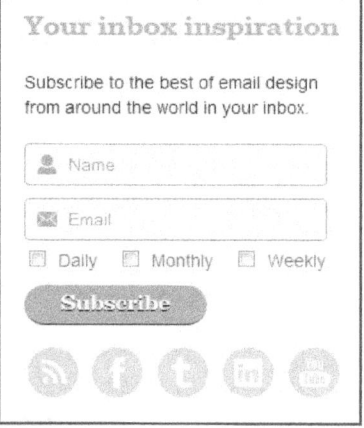

On the right is a better example of a subscribe form, where it only asks for the core information, but you could probably increase subscriptions on this form by providing a preview of the type of email the subscriber will get and giving a reason why someone would want to subscribe.

2. **Ask in blog posts.**
   A source of great, engaged subscribers is adding a subscribe form to the end of an article or blog post you wrote. At this point, the reader is very engaged, knows the quality of your content, and most likely wants to receive more in the future.

3. **Ask on social networks.**
   As we have seen in the marketing mix, use the different social networks as a channel to build your subscriber lists. Put a link or offer on those social networking channels where a reader can subscribe on your website. Also, do not forget to add a link to your email signature.

4. **Ask offline too.**
   When someone walks into your business, phones you, makes a booking, or you meet them at an event, ask them if you can keep them updated in the future. Train your staff to ask for this as well, and have it part of any forms visitors or customers must use. I've found that asking people face-to-face will increase later opens and interactions via email with that person.

5. **Ask current and past customers.**
   These are people who have already proven they will pay you money. Existing customers are your strongest leads for the future. Hang onto them with anything you've got. It costs 6-7 times more to obtain new customers than to retain existing ones.

6. **Offer something.**
   A hotel put together a guide for attractions in the local area for guests and put it online as a downloadable guide. People searching online for local attractions would find this guide, subscribe and download it, and the hotel started building a subscriber list of interested people looking forward to visiting the area.

7. **Run a competition.**
   There is no point in running a competition with your own customers and subscribers. Advertise the competition, or team up with another business which has a similar customer base to yourself, but might not be in direct competition.

   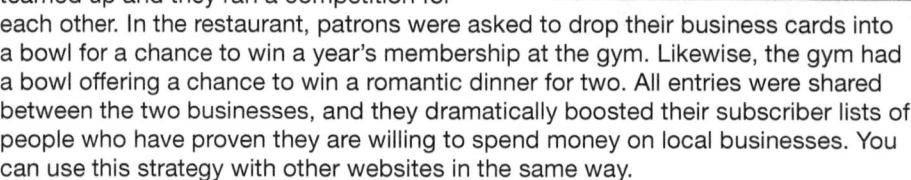

   For example, a local gym and restaurant teamed up and they ran a competition for each other. In the restaurant, patrons were asked to drop their business cards into a bowl for a chance to win a year's membership at the gym. Likewise, the gym had a bowl offering a chance to win a romantic dinner for two. All entries were shared between the two businesses, and they dramatically boosted their subscriber lists of people who have proven they are willing to spend money on local businesses. You can use this strategy with other websites in the same way.

8. **Run a course.**
   Seth Godin, in his book The Purple Cow, has a great story about a wine merchant who changed his traditional advertising to build a subscriber list. Instead of his usual newspaper advert with wine specials of the week, he instead advertised an email-based wine appreciation course. He took the detailed information about the wine that was already being supplied to him by wholesale

   suppliers and vineyards. He then compiled it into an enjoyable ten week course, sending one email a week.

   The response to the advert was fantastic, and the business results were even better. First, he didn't have to write the content; it was already being supplied to him. He got a huge number of signups from people interested in learning about wine. As they learned, they were excited to show off their knowledge to friends and family, and of course, the wine merchant was the obvious place to buy the wine. At the end of the course, he had his own list of customers he could advertise to again and again for a fraction of the cost of a single press advert.

   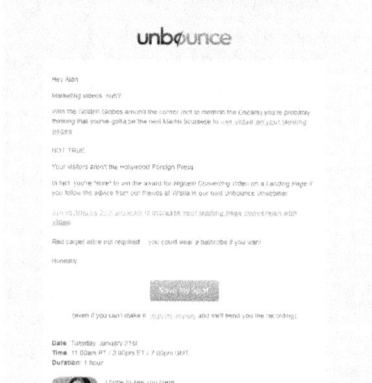

9. **Partner with other organisations.**
   You can team up with other websites and run a course on their website. Here, you can see the video hosting service Wistia have partnered with the landing page service unbounce.com to offer a webinar about using video to convert customers. Both parties would expect to share subscribers.

10. **Create a free tool or resource.**
    One wedding company created a one-page web application called whenismywedding.com. Here, future brides and grooms could create a web banner or ticker that would automatically count down the days to their own wedding. They would then share the banner on their own websites, Facebook, forums, and email.

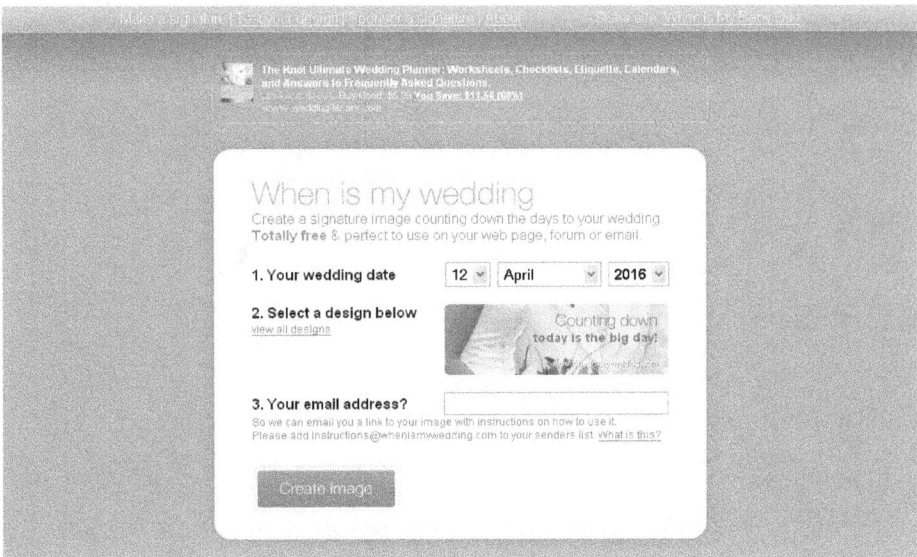

At the end of the setup process, the bride or groom was asked if they wanted to receive a regular email with wedding tips. This free tool generated over 50,000 email addresses in one year. We will see later what type of information you should ask from subscribers to get better results from your email campaigns.

MarketingSherpa.com surveyed 1,100 marketers not just about which strategy pulled in the most email addresses but which brought in the highest quality leads. Notice on the next page how the highest quality leads comes at the point where a person is most engaged with a business.

Which of the following strategies can you use for building your email subscriber list?

The most effective tactics for building subscriber lists

Tactic	Percentage
Website registration page	77%
Social media sharing buttons	48%
Offline events	47%
Registration during purchase	41%
Online events	39%
Facebook registration page	34%
Email to a friend	31%
Paid search	29%
Blog registration page	28%
Co-registration programs	12%
Other	6%

Source: MarketingSherpa.com

4. SPAM

Let's talk about permission.
Each country has its own particular laws on this issue, or is on the way to getting them. You will need to check with the data protection office in your own country to get the exact definition. However, you and the law no longer get to decide if your email is spam; this button here decides, and you do not get to debate the issue.

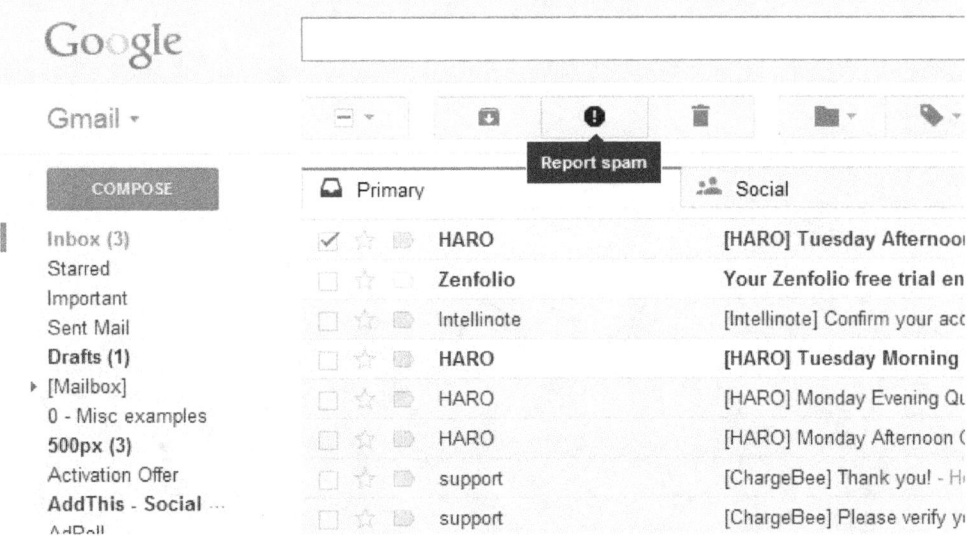

Every email client has a big button where the person receiving the mail makes that decision. If enough people click this button, all your emails, including your legitimate emails to clients and friends, will automatically be sent to the spam folder. And you will not get a say in the matter.

A previous client of mine tried the spam route in a previous life, and the amazing thing is, it worked – for a while. He started a dating site. A great business; low maintenance and pretty much runs itself generating revenue. Now, the problem with dating sites is to attract enough customers. To attract customers, you need lots of potential dates in the database, but you can't get dates in the database without having dates in the database, and no one is going to pay for an

empty dating site. It's a vicious circle. So, he took what seemed the obvious and easy route, and bought a list of one million email addresses, and he sent each person an email.

The response rate was about one percent, which was fantastic. Instantly, he had a database of a few thousand dates and the business was up and running. But then, the complaints started. Blog and forum posts about the spamming warned people to stay clear of this company. These sites and blogs were around a lot longer than my client's site, so these sites ranked above his listing in the search results. In the end, the effect was devastating and the site had to close. Now, the client is not a bad guy. He didn't think it was spam, just a great offer. The people who responded thought it was a great offer. Who knows, maybe some of them even found love, got married, had kids. However, enough people thought it was spam to bring the business to its knees.

Spam is in the eye of the beholder.

Forget about what you think of your email. Remember what the receiver will think. Any doubts? Do not send.

Before you hit send, make sure you are covered legally and read the rules for your country here: https://en.wikipedia.org/wiki/Email_spam_legislation_by_country

Worksheet step 2

Now, it's time to pause and take a moment and look back over the ten ideas for getting subscribers. Have a look which of these would be applicable to your business. Every business and organisation is different, so look at where you interact with your customers for opportunities. Take ten minutes, come up with ten ideas, and when you come back we will look at content for your email newsletters.

Two types of email

5. Email one: Retention

So, here's the problem: you have a wonderful website, but it's not generating enough sales for your business. Take heart, you are not alone. It is estimated that 80 percent of your site's visitors will never return. We're all busy, we need a little reminding about your services now and then.

So, what do you do to encourage your visitors and past customers back? A regular newsletter is the solution to connect with them. Begin an ongoing relationship with them and keep them coming back again and again. I call this the "I'm not dead" email. But what can you write about? Your subscribers have already given you the first clue by declaring their interests when they subscribed: what page or content they were reading when they signed up, and what they purchased from you. Good, interesting content is not hard to find with a little thought.

Remember the wine merchant idea earlier? He used free information provided to him to create a wine appreciation course. Newsletter by newsletter, he explained the virtues and characteristics of wines in his shop, and along with that he gained the trust and confidence of would-be purchasers. The information he gave them was free and was provided by winemakers, not himself. But the upshot? He became known in his locality as an authority on wine. He converted readers to purchasers and ultimately grew his business.

Like our wine merchant, think of the expertise you have in your field, and see how you can repackage it for your subscribers. Keep it simple and relevant to the needs of your clients. Here are a few more ideas for content you can send to your subscribers:

1. Think of seasonal messages. Seasonal messages are a great reason to get in touch with subscribers, and almost every single day in the year is covered. The big ones, of course, are Christmas, Thanksgiving, New Year's, Valentine's, St. Patrick's Day, Halloween, Independence Day, and many more, but you also have more obscure and whacky days such as National Talk in an Elevator Day, Talk like a Pirate Day, or you could do what Dunkin' Donuts did and create a National Donut Day. Don't forget the personal holidays, such as birthdays, wedding anniversaries, or the anniversary of the day they first signed up to your service.

2. Think about how-to guides. How-to guides are a great form of content, as they are very useful to subscribers, and position you as an expert in your industry. If you or your team get the same support queries from customers or the same questions from prospects over and over again, use those answers to create a step-by-step guide. Instead of a full guide, you could pick out a selection of insider, expert tips from your team, and share those instead.

3. Try surveying your customers, their customers, and others in your industry. Ask how they work, or their opinion on various opportunities in the future. Compile a buyer's guide, comparing prices and features of a certain type of service or product.

4. Interview someone or tell their story. Interview experts in the industry, interview your team, interview clients, or have your team interview you. If you do not want to write it, then video it or record the audio on Skype, , then put the interview in your e-mail newsletter.

5. Why not aggregate and curate industry news. Let me tell you about Sarah (not her real name). Sarah is currently regarded as an expert in her field. She regularly gets invited to talk at conferences around the world, chair panels, and she has some of the biggest companies in the world as her clients. She did this by positioning herself as the leading source of news in her industry, even though she never writes a word of it herself. Sarah will admit it to you: she hates writing, which is why she chose this strategy. It's pretty simple. Sarah subscribes to the top websites and industry leaders in her sector. Daily, for about 20 minutes, she scans the latest news, takes the heading and a small snippet of interesting news and copies it into her blog along with a link back to the source. Then, once a day, her blog posts of the latest news are automatically pulled into an e-mail newsletter and sent to an ever-growing list of subscribers.

Again, Sarah writes none of it, but people subscribe to get a handy summary of all the important industry news in one place. The people whose news or articles she features love it, because she brings them lots of traffic and new readers, and Sarah herself is seen as the leading figure in the industry, with all the latest information. Why not do this for your subscribers?

6. Why not try top 10 lists? This is a content strategy that most of the entertainment channels use. Think "top 10 celebrity meltdowns", "top 100 comedy moments on TV", or "the top 10 sites to read in your industry".

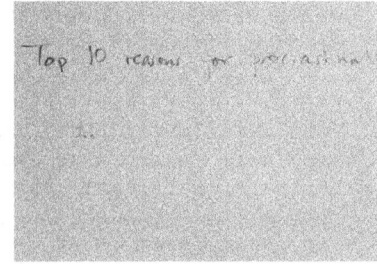

7. Even something as simple as finding something fun or interesting on the internet and sharing it with your subscribers works. I know the head of a marketing firm who sends an email every two weeks and finishes it with a link to a fun story, video, or image on the web. It is the most viewed and shared part of the email, and ensures the email always gets opened.

8. Share what you've learned or what your team has learned. Share the top five things you have learned at a recent conference, event, or even from a book you've read.

9. Why not recycle some old content? Take last year's content and turn it into a different format. Take an article and turn it into a video, infographic, eBook or course. Collect together articles in the same category and create a reference guide.

10. And if you really can't write, you can design it. A sports clothing company I worked with had an abundance of design talent but no one on the staff to do writing, so we came up with the strategy to utilise that skill for some unique content. We looked at ways of converting existing content into a new visual format. Every sport has some brilliant quotes, from the smart to the funny, and sometimes just bizarre. The team took those text and audio quotes, and designed them. The result was unique and a great success that even spawned a mobile app and book. Subscribers would sign up to get a new sporting quote in their inbox every week, and the company would also feature other products in the mail. Is there existing content in your industry that you can use?

11. Marketing software firm Moz.com takes a difficult or complex concept and every Friday does a quick video in front of a whiteboard, where the concept is explained and illustrated. It's very low tech and you can do this with a camera phone and a whiteboard. A quick tip from my days studying film in college; people are more forgiving about bad quality video than bad quality sound.

Here are some quick content dos and don'ts:

Do:
- Keep it short and sweet. Too little is better than too much. On average, keep your content around 300 words. Any longer than that, try and link it out to your website.

- Be personal, be honest, and give your opinion.

- Show some of your personality. People connect better with people.

- Use images that go with your newsletter. They brighten it up, making it much more visually interesting. Images can help break up your text and make your email easier to read, and images can also direct your reader to your main call to action. There are plenty of great online image libraries that you can use, with images as cheap as one dollar.

Don't:
- Send irrelevant content. You'll just annoy customers.

- And definitely do not send large attachments. I spent half an hour last week downloading an email from a local restaurant on my phone, only to find it was their menu. I was not impressed. So, if you have to send something big send a link to a website instead where someone can download it.

Worksheet step 3

Now, let's take a moment to brainstorm ten types of content you could send to your subscribers. If you're sending an email newsletter every month, you will now have a plan covering the next ten months. Remember, it must be interesting and engaging.

6. Designing emails for results

Let's talk about designing for results. Some people prefer plain text emails, while others prefer a few visual bells and whistles. If you're approaching email for marketing purposes, according to research, it's a no-brainer. People simply respond better to HTML-designed emails. If you compare the two side by side, the strength of the design becomes more obvious. Would you prefer newsletter one or does newsletter two grab more attention?

The actual figure is that HTML-designed emails perform on average 200% better than their plain text alternatives.

Another consideration when designing for email is that you need to design for no images. The bad news is that designing and coding for email is a lot more complicated than a webpage. Instead of three or four main web browsers, such as Internet Explorer, Firefox, Safari, or Opera, you have over 20 different email clients your subscribers could be using. Each of these will have their own quirks and support—or lack of—for different design elements. For example, in most email clients, images are turned off by default. A user has to either turn on images for your email or add you to their contacts list, where you're deemed safe and images are turned on. So, you need to make sure to design your email so that if there are no images it can still be understood by the reader.

Here's an example where images off doesn't work very well.

Here's another example from Pizza Express that is designed really well. You can see that even with images off, the email performs very well and can be clearly read and understood.

To design for images off, use the following steps:

- Ensure you have a link at the top of your email to a web-based version of the email, so subscribers can view it in a web browser.

- Use text as much as possible, but you do not have to go mad and make everything text. Use text where you can, and use images where a design will really help your message.

- Use alternative text for your important images. For example, you can see here the word "pizza" is one image. When it is not displayed, the HTML ALT text "pizza" is also displayed.

- Use blocks of colour to differentiate different areas, but be sure that the URL text, which is by default blue in many email clients, can still be read on the background colour.

- You can test how your email looks in different email clients. Two great tools for testing emails are litmus.com and emailonacid.com. There, you can send your email newsletter to these services, and they will give you back screenshots of how it looks in every major email client with and without images.

- You can also get design inspiration online if you search "beautiful email newsletters" in google. You should get back some good ideas to try.

For examples of email design check out http://www.beautiful-email-newsletters.com/

7. How to send - ESPs

ESPs or Email Service Providers are dedicated tools specifically designed to send and track email newsletters and subscribers.
You can of course send your own newsletters from Outlook or Gmail, but if you use dedicated email and marketing software, you get a wealth of great features to make your life easier and faster. If you get anywhere near 100 subscribers, you realise that normal email clients such as Outlook and Gmail are just not up to the task. More impossible is if you want to personalise each email. Thankfully, these email tools take all the hard work out of it.

Here are some of the great standard features you get with most email services:

- **Subscriber management.**
  From giving you the email capture form to put on your site, to allowing your user to unsubscribe themselves via a link at the bottom of your emails.

- **Email templates.**
  Many services provide a range of good quality, professional-looking email templates at no additional cost, and allow you to make edits to them via an inbuilt editor. Once you have your email template ready to go, you can go in each week or month and update the text and images yourself via an easy-to-use editor.

- **Personalisation.**
  Let the computer do the hard work of starting every email with the person's name. For example, "Hello, John." You can get really fancy and customise entire sections of an email based on a user's preference.

- **Sending and delivery.**
  Regular email communication is not as reliable as you might think. A large chunk of email every day never reaches its destination, or can end up in a spam folder. Most email services use a variety of systems to ensure your email is not viewed as spam and lands in your subscriber's inbox.

- **Tracking.**
  With an email marketing tool, you can track which of your subscribers has opened an email, when, what they clicked on, and if they unsubscribed. We will cover tracking later in this module.

The feature sets of the top players are pretty similar. Your preference will come down to which tool you find easiest to use, and has the best pricing model that suits your business. For example, some online systems charge a monthly subscription, starting at 10 dollars for up to 500 subscribers, while others work on a pay-as-you-go model of 0.01 cent per subscriber.

8. How often to send

So, we've talked about subscribers: where to get them and how to get them, and we've talked about content ideas that you can send to the subscribers. The next biggest question is how often to send your emails.

I'm sorry but there is no single answer to this and anyone who says there is should be avoided. Every industry and organisation has their own seasons and timeframes. What works for one industry may not work for yours. The best thing to do is to test it. If you feel you need to send frequently, then try sending each week. If not, monthly may be better, but monitor the number of people who unsubscribe from the email, and watch for any issues. Whatever frequency you discover is best for your audience, make sure you stick to it. It's all about building trust and reliability.

The two most common issues I see around frequency are sending too often and sending too little. Both are as bad as each other and damaging to your list.

1. Too often and people get annoyed and unsubscribe.

2. Too little and people forget they subscribed, marking your emails as spam.

Most people send too little. Keep testing sending more and more frequently and closely monitor your unsubscribe rate after each send. Your users will quickly tell you when is too much.

Worksheet step 4

Decide on how often and what day you are going to send your email. At this stage it is OK to guess. Then start testing sending your email more frequently until you begin to see an increase in unsubscribes. Test sending your email on different days of the week and in the morning and afternoon. Do not avoid testing on a Sunday as you will have a lot less competition in a subscriber's inbox on this day.

9. Checklist for sending your first mail newsletter

1. **Sign up to an email service provider (ESP).**
   There are lots of available services. CampaignMonitor.com and MailChimp.com are two such services but whatever you decide ensure it has the following functionality: Sending and delivery, Tracking, Subscribers list management, Unsubscribe and personalisation.

2. **Create a subscriber list.**
   Name it something you will remember, e.g., "Subscribers from my website homepage" or "Customers from this year".

3. **Add subscribers.**
   You should be able to upload a list of subscribers to your list. Their email address is the most important but also try to include their name so you can personalise your emails to them with "Hi NAME" Ensure you have permission from these people to email them. If you are not sure, ask them.
   If you do not, yet have a list of subscribers, you can create a form in your ESP that you can then add to your website. The form can offer a free download or a weekly news update to viewers if they add their details to the form.
   Note: Refer to chapter 3, Getting Subscribers, for ideas on how to get subscribers.

4. **Create your first email campaign.**
   Give it a name you can read in a year's time and understand what it was for. For example "Monthly newsletter April, this year" or "50% off sales campaign selling X product".
   Be clear on the purpose of the email. Ask yourself if the reader does only one thing after reading this email what should it be?
   Add who the email is coming from (a personal name at YourCompany is better than just YourCompany).
   And add the email address that you want the email to come from and let subscribers reply to this.

5. **Email design.**
   You can upload your own ready made email design or you can use one of the templates provided by the email service.
   If you google "free / paid email templates" you can find a range of great designs if the ones from the email service are not to your liking.
   Some email services provide an editor for templates. If yours does not you will need to get someone comfortable programming in HTML to make the changes to the template for you.

   Note: Refer to chapter 6, Email Design, to see how companies work with images on and off. www.beautiful-email-newsletters.com is a handy online gallery of the best in email design for inspiration.

6. Email content.

Add your content. Again most services have an inbuilt content editor, especially if you use one of their ready made templates. However if they do not you will have to edit the code (HTML) of the newsletter yourself to add it.

Ensure your content is engaging, short and sweet. If it is a sales email make sure it clearly states the proposition and has one clear call to action.

Use images to both engage the reader, split up longer content and support the content. But if you do use images make sure the email still works with images turned off.

If you are also sending a plain text version of the email try and format the text to make each section clear and readable.

Note: Refer to chapter 5, Retention, for content ideas and content dos and don'ts.

7. Testing

Send the email to yourself and your team to read, test how it looks in different email clients such as Outlook, Gmail, Yahoo etc and ensure all the links work.

Note: You can also use a service like Litmus.com and emailonacid.com to test how the email looks in all email clients.

8. Send.

If all looks good after testing. Send the email to your subscriber list(s). You should quickly get a report back on how many people opened your email and what they clicked on.

Using this report craft your next email to get more people to open it (better subject line or offer?), read it (What was the most popular article last month?) and take action (What was the most popular link clicked?).

Congratulations you have sent your first email newsletter!

10. Email two - The sales email

The second key type of email newsletter to send is the sales email. Remember our marketing loop earlier in the presentation? The sales email takes the user out of that loop with the specific intention of getting them to perform an action or make a purchase. Whether they buy or don't buy, it's important to maintain a good relationship and bring them back to your regular newsletters with the hope that they will buy from you again in the future. According to internetretailer.com, over four times as many survey responders prefer to receive promotions via email rather than social media.

Over four times as many survey responders prefer to receive promotions via email rather than social media. internetretailer.com

Let's break down a typical email campaign and the type of numbers you should expect. Let's take an example of a consulting firm, with an hourly rate of 100 dollars for their services. The firm, and John, the CEO, have built up a subscriber list of 1000 people. They have been emailing that list once a month, keeping them updated on the firm's activities, so the list is active and engaged.

John emails the list with a great offer of a new service. He first tests the offer with different subject lines and different images in each email. He sends version A of the email to 100 subscribers, and version B to a different 100 people. Tracking tools will show John who opened and clicked on which email.

Whichever email gets the best number of opens, or even better, the most number of clicks to the buy page, will get used and be sent to the remaining 800 subscribers.

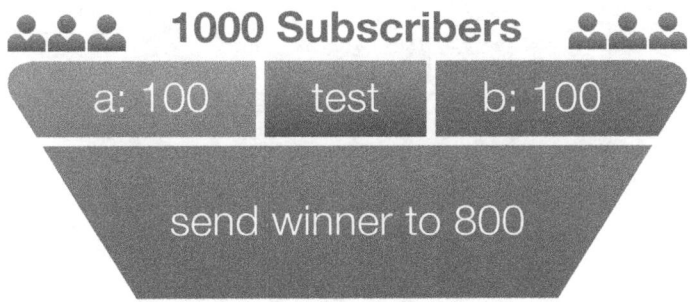

John would expect around about 25 percent of subscribers, or 200 people to open and read the email.
MailChimp.com have a great resource breaking down the average open rates and click rates by industry. It's worth checking their website to see how your email newsletter compares to the industry average.

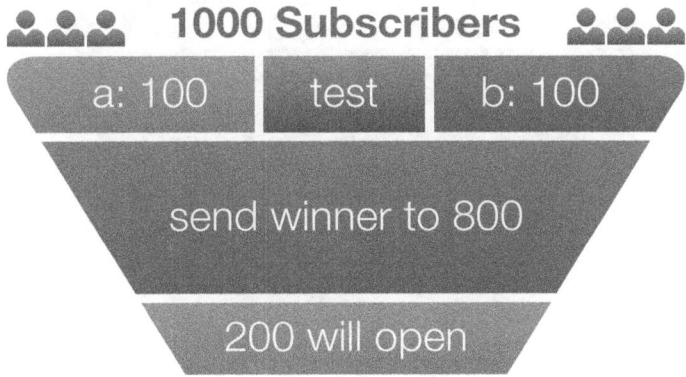

Of the 200 people who have read the email, about eight would be interested enough in the offer to click through to an order page to find out more.

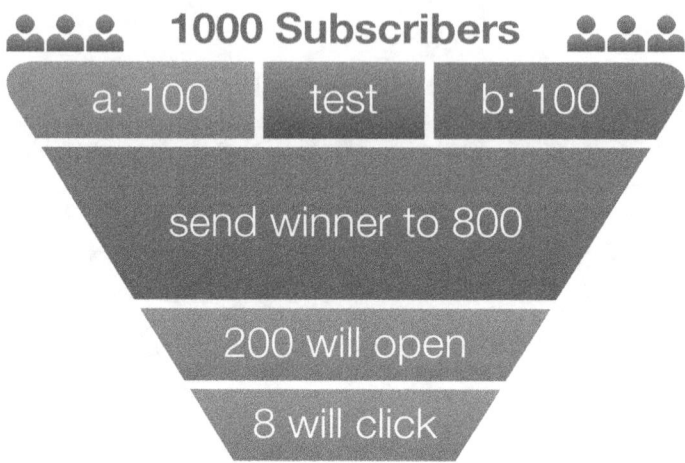

Of those eight, on average one person would complete the order process and purchase what John is selling.

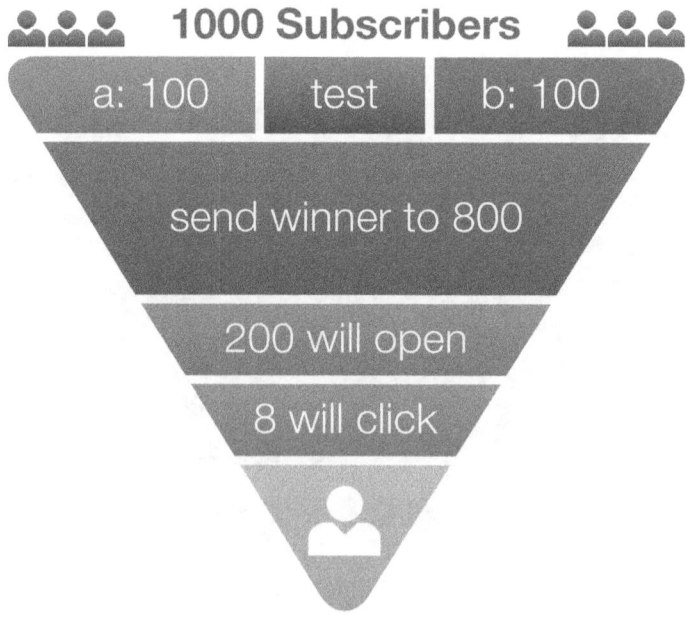

Now, at this point, one purchase looks like a bad number, but wait. The cost of sending the emails to John's email list of 1000 subscribers was $10 (cost of sending via a common ESP), but John has just sold about 8 hours of consulting service, totalling 800 dollars. That is a great return on investment. But wait, it gets better. Remember the 600+ people who have not opened the email? John can email them again at a different time or day. These people will not get annoyed, as they didn't get to read John's first email, and there's a 50 percent likelihood that John can generate another sale out of this second email.

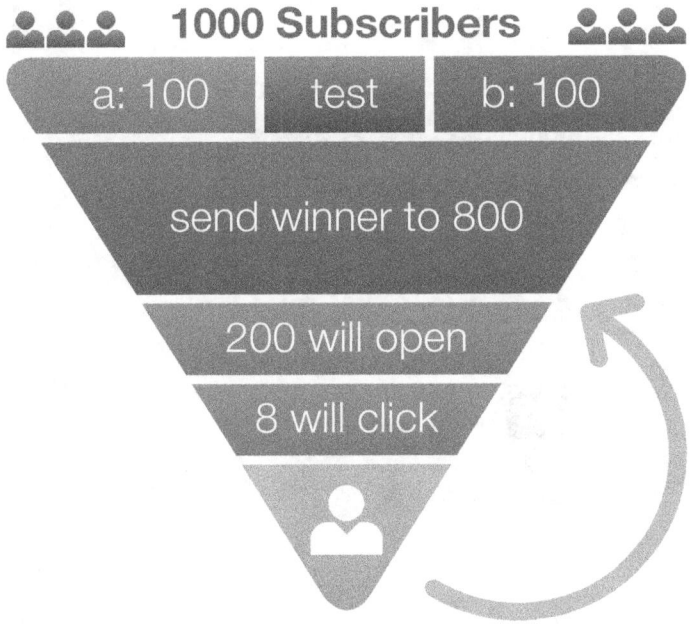

11. Anatomy of a newsletter

Let's look at the anatomy of a monthly email newsletter:

1. **Subject line.**
   Your very first point of contact. Use this to tempt the reader to open the mail. I add the company name to every subject line, to build trust over time. Readers learn that if the mail is from my company, then there will be something inside they will find interesting or enjoyable. In this example the company is a sports T-shirt company.

2. **Preview.**
   This text will appear in the preview pane of the email client when it arrives in the inbox. It should add to the subject line and provide more reasons to open the newsletter.

A reader should be in no doubt what to do next, and why.

3. **Main offer.**
   A clear offer with a strong call to action. A reader should be in no doubt what to do next, and why. Fancy fonts here will need to be images, so make sure you have text and images that work when images are turned off.

4. **Sell stuff.**
   Don't forget that your ultimate goal is to sell your products or services.

5. **Be useful.**
   Subscribers would get turned off pretty fast if every mail was an offer, or about me. I always add content I know would be of use to a subscriber. It increases the chance of them opening again next month.

6. **Expand the conversation.**
   People love sharing good links and information online. With an army of subscribers loving your updates, make it easy for them to tell others and shout back to you.

7. **Reminder.**
   A personal touch to let them know you're human, and a simple reminder of where they signed up. This can drastically reduce the numbers who unsubscribe, but if they want to go, let them.

8. **Short and sweet.**
   I like to keep my newsletters short and easy to scan. If I have a long article, I split it into a snappy taster for the newsletter and a "read more" link going to the blog.

That's all. If you start applying these points to your email marketing campaigns, you will see your open rates and click-through rates start to rise.

12. Landing pages

Image © KissMetrics

Kissmetrics have a great post on landing page basics at https://blog.kissmetrics.com/landing-page-design-infographic/. When you are doing a sales campaign, you're most likely directing the user to a web page, where they will make a purchase decision and click "Buy". This is called a landing page.

Ensure you use a dedicated landing page for every campaign you do. Do not send the customer to your home page. Home pages are designed to give readers an overview of your business, people, products, and an introduction to the different sections of your website. A landing page is designed to encourage the reader to perform one specific task, usually buy something. There is nothing worse than spending loads of time and money on an email campaign, only to see the purchase abandoned when they hit your landing page and get distracted.

Landing page optimisation and testing is a big subject to cover, but here are the top 10 things to look out for:

1. Ideally the headline of your landing page should match the headline or call to action of your advert. The last thing you want is a lead second guessing if they are on the right page.

2. Make sure your heading is clear and concise. There should be absolutely no doubt that this is the page they are looking for and it is worth reading more.

3. I'm terrible at spelling and grammar. As a result I always ensure anything I write goes through at least two different editors and a spell check. If you are asking people to hand over money to you then you need to look professional and detail orientated. Any doubt at all will result in people not buying.

4. Which do you trust more? If I say I am great or if others say I am great? We trust others more don't we? Leverage that by adding testimonials, press, customer logos and badges to your page to appear more trustworthy.

5. Have a clear, strong call to action. Ideally it should tie in to the headline you used and make it clear what happens next.

6. Your button / call to action should jump out on the screen. Use a vibrant colour that jumps out from the page. Ideally when a user scans the page it should be clear what to click for the next step.

7. Remove any non-essential links. Every link you have on the page is another distraction to bring the user away from clicking the buy button.

8. Show don't tell. Use images and video to show what you are selling or to tell your story better. Faces will always catch a reader's eye but make sure that the face you use is turned and looking to your main call to action. A reader will follow that eye path.

9. Try and keep everything important above the fold so that people do not have to scroll to see your main call to action. People do scroll on websites but this does help cut out a step for the user.

10. Test. Once you have a page live, start testing alternative versions with different images, headings and calls to action.

The headline of your landing page should match the headline or call to action of your advert.

13. Tracking and analysis

There is a huge amount of information and subscriber behaviour you can track in email marketing, and if you can track it, you can improve it. Let's look at a campaign report.

All good email service providers provide tracking tools which are essential if you want to build and improve your marketing efforts. This is a typical reporting screen for an ESP called campaignmonitor.com, but will look very similar in other tools.

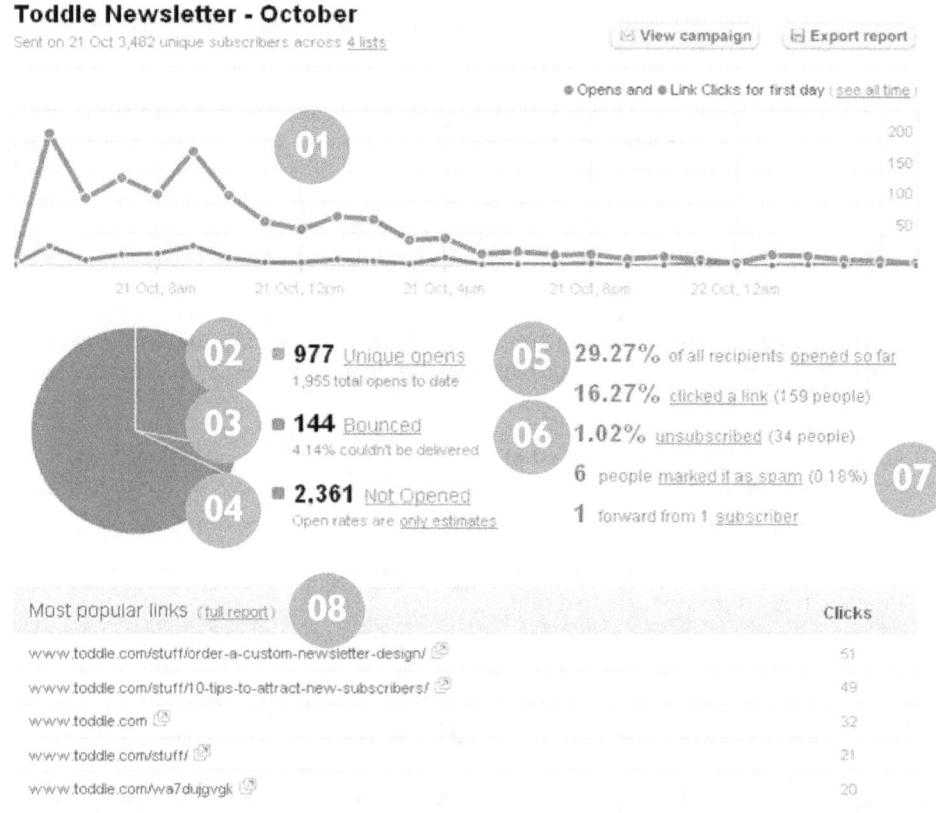

1. The graph shows the performance of an email over a couple of days after the email was sent. It shows the number of people who opened the email and clicked the link within it.

2. You can see how many people opened the email and how many times.

3. This number is how many emails could not be delivered or 'bounced'.
Some people leave jobs and companies close, so some emails no longer work. In

fact up to 30% of the emails in your list can go dead after a year. It is a good idea to regularly clean out dead emails from your database. If you are seen to be regularly sending emails to lots of dead email addresses over a long time, inboxes could start to view your emails as spam. However, most of the email service providers will automatically remove dead email addresses if they continue to bounce, which will save you a lot of hassle.

4. It's important to note that the opened numbers here are a sample, and not the full picture. This is because emails are tracked in two ways. Firstly, to track if an email is opened, the email software puts in an invisible image. When this image is displayed in a subscriber's inbox, the software tracks that as an open. However, as we read earlier, some email clients and users do not display images in the inbox. So, while a subscriber might have read the email, the tracking software will not know. Secondly, the email software changes the links in an email to redirect through their software. This way, the software can track both the subscriber, what they clicked, and how many times they clicked. With any of these stats, you can click in to see a more detailed report of what an individual subscriber did.

5. These two numbers (% of opened and % of clicked) are commonly used to track the success of an email but can be a distraction if you are sending a sale email. Ultimately the number who clicked the "buy" link is the most important. See point 8. This number, combined with your sales figures which you can track back to the campaign, tells you how well the email is doing. If you find that you are getting a high click rate, but ultimately very little sales, it could indicate that you need to improve the landing or checkout pages, or you're not providing enough information in the email for a subscriber to make a decision.

6. Unsubscribes. This is your first warning number. You should always expect a few people to unsubscribe. People, circumstances, and interests change all the time, and your content and business may no longer be relevant to them. However, if this number starts to go up, then it may mean you're sending out the wrong type of content and offers. You may be sending out emails too frequently, or you may be attracting the wrong subscribers in the first place.

7. This is your second warning number, and you need to keep it below 0.3 percent before the email service provider's automatic warnings kick in and you face a potential ban. What this number indicates is that when a user received your email in Gmail, Hotmail, Yahoo or others, they clicked the spam button. A user can do this for a variety of reasons. They might simply not remember who you are or subscribing to your newsletter which is why it's always a good idea to email subscribers frequently. If you do not email frequently, add a small reminder to the email about how they initially subscribed to your service and who you are. A user might also simply want to stop receiving your newsletter, but did not see an obvious way to unsubscribe. It is important to make it obvious to a subscriber how to remove themselves from your list, or change how often they receive emails.

8. And finally, you can see the most popular links that subscribers clicked on in your email. Ideally, the most clicked link should be your intended call to action.

14. Measuring ROI

If you want to measure the return on investment for your email or any marketing activity, you can use the following calculation:

Take your money earned, subtract from that the money spent, including your time, and divide that by the money spent, including your time.

$$\frac{\text{Earned} - \text{Spent}}{\text{Spent}} = \text{ROI}$$

The resulting figure is your percentage return on investment. Or to describe that in English, take all the money your email campaign has just earned, e.g. number of sales, new clients, subtract from that the money you spent on the campaign, and divide it by the money you just spent on the campaign. The final figure is your return on investment. So for example if you earned $1000 in sales and you spend $500 to run the campaign you will have return on investment of 100%.

$$\frac{1000 - 500}{500} = \%100$$

Make sure to include your own time in this calculation. Note that if you're not sure of your hourly rate, take your annual income and divide it by 2080 hours.

$$\frac{\text{Annual income}}{2,080} = \text{Hourly rate}$$

$$\text{Hours} \times \text{Rate} = \text{Time Spent}$$

Now of course, the final return on investment figure should be more than zero. If it is less than zero you need to change or stop what you are doing.

Worksheet step 5

What will you track to measure if your email was a success?

15. Segmenting subscribers

If there's only one thing you do with your email lists, segment your users into tastes, events, dates, anything you can to narrow them down into particular groups. It is one of the most powerful and underused aspects of email marketing. The tighter you can target your email newsletters, the better your emails will perform.

Here is an example of segmenting in use by the online sports T-shirt shop Sheepstealers. Sheepstealers grabbed a date of birth when John was signing up and tracked his purchasing history to see what team he supports. Now every year Sheepstealers sends John an email before his birthday with gift ideas he can share with his family or to treat himself. It also includes helpful last order dates to ensure John gets his gifts in time.

All it takes to make this sale every year is an email. This is what makes segmentation the most powerful marketing tool you have. At its simplest, segmentation is getting more data on your customers so you can better target them based on their likes and dislikes.

Looking at the example of the sports T-shirt retailer, when getting a subscriber to sign up, we ask for these key details:

- Name – If you can personalise the message with the prospect's name, it will greatly increase the number of opens and clicks, not to mention a reduction in the number of unsubscribes.

- Email address – this is the absolute basic and most important information.

Subscriber	John Doe
Email	John@email.com

And this is where most companies stop. Their next step is to add as many subscribers to that list and send them as many emails as possible.

But what if we added "favourite sports team" to the list of subscriber details? This we decided is the absolute basic information required to make the email program work.

The team information is the first step in segmentation. From this, we can ensure each person would only get an email for the team they support and will not be annoyed with irrelevant information about other teams, ensuring they will open again and again, each time. This also provides business intelligence back to the product team. For example, if team A has 2,000 subscribers, and team B has ten subscribers, then we can spend time producing more products targeting team A.

You should build deep instead of wide. By that I mean you can often make more sales by getting more information and better targeting of existing subscribers instead of acquiring more subscribers. Now you have an interested subscriber. What if you work to add more details to their profile? You don't always have to annoy subscribers by asking. With a bit of programming and hidden fields in your form, you can detect what

Subscriber	John Doe
Email	John@email.com
Your County / Team	Meath
Your Birthday	9 January 1976
Address	Bettystown
Country	Ireland

country a user is subscribing from, or what site referred them before they signed up. For example, you might see that 50 percent of your subscribers are from outside of your country. Maybe it's time to adjust your advertising strategy to better target that country. If you see that three times as many people subscribe to your email and they come from Facebook, now you know where to concentrate more of your marketing efforts. In fact, most of the information on this screen is what Facebook asks for when targeting your advertising on their network.

Subscriber	John Doe
Email	John@email.com
Your County / Team	Meath
Your Birthday	9 January 1976
Address	Bettystown
Country	Ireland
Previously Purchased	Yes
Age	40
Sex	Male
Where did you hear of us?	Facebook
Source of signup	Facebook
Status	Active
Joined list	30 April

How to get more subscriber details.
How else can you get more information?

- Ask. Ask each subscriber to add their own details so you can send them more relevant information or offers. Run a competition or other incentives to fill out more details about themselves.

- Internet marketer Chris Penn (christopherspenn.com) added a premium content section to his email newsletter. Only those who complete their profile information get to see the premium section, and a large percentage of subscribers happily did this.

- Tell subscribers you will send them a birthday gift. To get it, they need to give you their birthday and address.

- Another tip is to track what time a subscriber opens your email newsletter. Chances are, they will be there at the computer the same time next week or next month.

In summary, the more information you have on your subscriber and customer base, the more you can target your marketing. The more you target your marketing, the better the results you will get. People are happy to give you this information, but not all at once, and only in return for value. The added bonus of all this customer information is that it feeds back into the business and lets you tailor your products and your service to your customer's needs, or even spot gaps in the market.

The more you target your marketing, the better the results you will get.

Worksheet step 6

List ways you can group subscribers to better target content and offers to them in the future. Next, we'll take a look at automating your sales and marketing.

16. Automation

When a new subscriber gets added to your database or performs specific actions on your website, you can automatically send them an email newsletter. A simple example of this is when a user signs up, you can immediately send them a welcome mail. I use it when giving away a sample chapter of my book. A user must sign up to get a chapter. An autoresponder will then send them a thank you and a link to download the book. I follow up this email in three days' time to ask what they thought of the book and ask if they would share their review on social media and Amazon. And lastly, I follow up again with a reminder to buy the book.

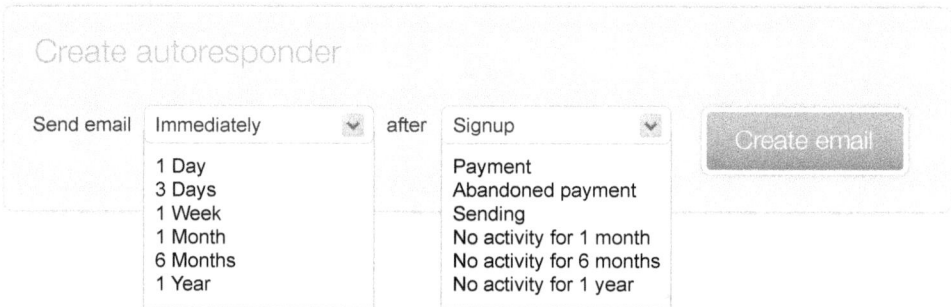

For the software application Toddle.com, we built our own autoresponder that could talk to our internal systems. It allowed us to automate emails to users, to ensure that they got the most out of our product and they stayed on and became paying customers. When a user signed up, they would get a welcome. If they paid, they would get a thank you, and sometimes an upsell to another product. If they abandoned the checkout, they would get a reminder to come back and finish. And if it looked like they would not come back, we would send out a special offer. And when a user stopped using the product for a certain amount of time, they would get a reminder to come back and we sent them a new newsletter. It was really effective for the business and users appreciated the care and attention we seemed to give them. Now with new tools like Intercom.io you no longer need to build your own system.

Autoresponders are fundamental to the growth of many successful online companies. In particular, they are used to convert new users to customers in the most important 30 days after signup. A potential new customer's interest is at its peak when they first sign up to your service. It then quite dramatically drops off over the following 30 days if they do not start using it. Many companies create a sequence of emails to guide a user after signup towards purchase.

The following examples are from the online e-commerce platform Shopify, where you can create your own online shop. They send three automated emails over the course of a trial. Their first email is the welcome. It gets sent to the user immediately. It contains all the key getting started information a user might need to use the Shopify service.

Shopify have one of the nicer designed email sequences. It is great how they introduce your personal account manager Alex and devote a full third of the email to it. They sell the benefits of the service along with the next steps that they want you to take.

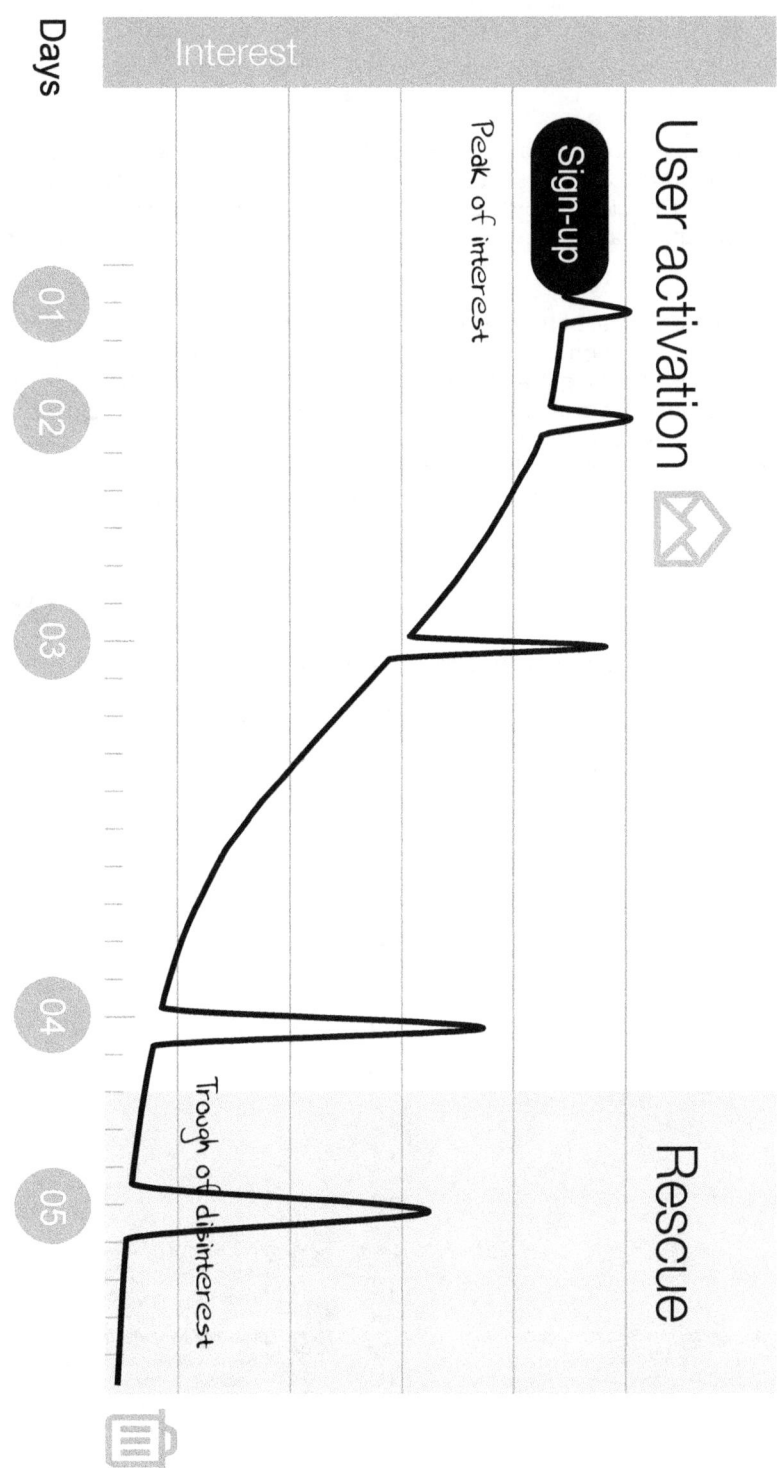

Twelve days later, just before your trial is due to expire, you get an email informing you of such, with options to purchase a plan. It also includes an extra incentive to sign up, with $100 of free Google AdWords credits. Shopify reinforce the personal touch here. You can phone and chat about what plan you should buy. Shopify know the power of real people.

The last automated email of the sequence gets sent on day 15 after your store has closed, with a call to action that it's still not too late; you can still purchase a plan. I like the extra hook of saying they have not yet deleted your data. The fear of losing something is a much more powerful driver of behaviour than the one to get something. This is one of their regular newsletters. You can see the types of content that they cover here. You can check out these sequences of emails, along with many others from different online companies from around the world in the book, 30 Days to Sell.

Shopify

E-commerce software, online store builder 14-day trial

 From: Shopify <mailer@shopify.com>
Date: Thu, Mar 21, at 6:19 PM
Subject: Welcome to Shopify

01 — day after sign-up
02
03
04
05
06
07
08
09
10
11
12
13
14

 From: Shopify <mailer@shopify.com>
Date: Thu, Apr 4, at 6:35 AM
Subject: Your online store has closed

15
16
17
18

 From: Shopify <mailer@shopify.com>
Date: Tue, Apr 2, at 9:27 AM
Subject: Your online store is about to close

 Monthly Newsletter
From: Shopify Newsletter <newsletter@shopify.com>
Date: Thu, Apr 4, at 10:18 PM
Subject: Get more online sales in April

Welcome to Shopify!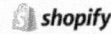

You've taken the first step towards world domination! Below you will find all of your account information, keep it in a safe place:

Your Store: http://beautifulben.myshopify.com

Your store is currently password protected using the password "droosk". You can remove the password protection when you're ready to launch your store.

Your Store's Admin Area: http://beautifulben.myshopify.com/admin/

If you ever forget your password, you can always recover it by clicking here.

Get ready for some sales!

We've built a step-by-step tutorial into your Store Admin to get you started. You can do the tutorial steps in any order, or skip them completely, it's up to you.

- Add Products
- Customize Your Design
- Add Content
- Getting Paid
- Setting Taxes
- Shipping Settings
- Domain Names

Meet your Shopify Guru!

We also provide every store owner with a personal Shopify Guru to help you make your store a success. Your Guru, Alex, can be reached via email at

alex.richards@shopify.com

Alex is available from Monday to Friday from 9am to 5pm EST.

The Shopify Guru Team

SUPPORT | FORUMS | THEME STORE | APP STORE | SHOPIFY EXPERTS | BLOG

© Shopify | 126 York Street, Ottawa, ON, K1N 5T5

Subject:
Welcome to Shopify

Sent:
Immediately

Call to action:
Get ready for some sales

Your store is about to close!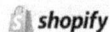

Hey beautifulben,

Your free Shopify trial will expire in less than 2 days! If you don't want your online store to be closed, please log in and pick a plan. If you have forgotten your password, you can easily recover it here.

Which Plan is Best for You?

Our friendly Sales Team would be happy to help you find the perfect plan for beautifulben. You can reach them by phone (1-888-SHOPIFY) or use our Sales Contact Form.

Get $100 in Credits Today

Pick a plan today and we'll give $100 in free credit for Google AdWords. You can use this to get customers to your online store.

Need Some Help?

Your Shopify Guru, Alex, is standing by to help you get your site up and running and an be reached via email at:

alex.richards@shopify.com

Alex is available from Monday to Friday from 9am to 5pm EST.

The Shopify Guru Team

SUPPORT | FORUMS | THEME STORE | APP STORE | SHOPIFY EXPERTS | BLOG

© Shopify | 126 York Street, Ottawa, ON, K1N 5T5

Subject:
Your online store is about to close

Sent:
Twelve days after signup.

Call to action:
Buy today
& get $100 google adwords credits.

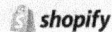

Subject:
Your online store has closed

Sent:
Fourteen days after signup

Call to action:
Re-open your store by picking a plan

Start selling more in April

Dear Alan O'Rourke,

Learning how to launch and grow your online store *can* be challenging. But it doesn't have to be! This month we're excited to announce the launch of Ecommerce University – a free resource to help you grow your business. We'll also tell you about our increased support coverage, pass on some great advice from our forums, and share two of this month's most popular themes.

Learn how to sell more online

Our freshly launched Ecommerce University is a collection of advice on how to sell online. You'll find ebooks, articles, videos, and discussion forums full of tips and tricks for beginners to experts alike — and it's all free.

Ecommerce University

Check out the new Ecommerce University.

Talk to us for free 24x7

We've expanded our customer service capacity to make sure you have the support you need, whenever you need it. Shopify gurus are always available to take your call or answer your email 24 hours a day, 7 days a week.

We also have toll-free and local phone numbers for:

UK: 0800 808 5233
Australia: 03 8400 4750
New Zealand: 07 788 6026
North America: 1 888 746 7439

The best of the forum

Our discussion forums are a place where you can ask questions and connect with other store owners. Here are some of this month's best conversations:

- How to price plus sized clothes
- Opinions on product prices
- Do I need a photographer?
- How do you get rid of old inventory?
- How to verify your Shopify website on Pinterest
- TV advertising: does anyone do it?
- Best tips for social media marketing

The best of the Shopify Blog

Our blog is filled with articles to help you build your business and sell more. Here are some of the most popular blog posts from the past month:

- New Shopify Apps to Help You Sell More
- 10 Must Know Image Optimization Tips
- All About US Trademarks
- Best of the Build-A-Business Mentor Tips

15

Monthly Newsletter

Subject:
Get more online sales in April

Sent:
Fourteen days after signup

Content
Business & marketing advice
Sell more in April
Learning resources
Free 24x7 support
Join our community
Our best blog posts
Try our theme store

Worksheet step 7

What portion of your email marketing can you automate?
Can you set op a series of emails to convert trial users to customers? Perhaps you can send a sequence of emails to people who download an eBook or resource from your website? Remember the email course from the wine merchant earlier in the book. You can automate that entire sequence of emails to send one every week for eight weeks. Every time a person subscribes they start on email one and automatically receive each mail every week.

17. Re-engaging old email lists

How I emailed a 'dead' list of 14,682 subscribers and only got 5 spam clicks and lots of love.

I would like to share a personal story from my blog on AudienceStack.com. From time to time during your marketing career you are going to inherit an old email list. This will be a bunch of subscribers who were collected but not emailed in a long while. You've been given the job of contacting them again. This is how I did it.

I took a big breath and my finger paused over the send button.
I was just about to send an email to 14,682 subscribers. Most of whom were not going to remember me or ever subscribing to my website. In fact the last email was sent to this email list well over a year and a half ago. The easiest choice for subscribers would be to mark this as spam, essentially killing the list. This needed to be handled delicately.

A labour of love

I started the email gallery site http://beautiful-email-newsletters.com (BEN) back in 2008, almost 7 years ago. That is old in internet years. The site started as a marketing site and lead generator for an email service provider (ESP) I founded. I eventually sold that company but held on to BEN as I still loved email and wanted to keep a hand in it. I also knew whatever I did next would be marketing related and having an audience would be a huge help. So for years I searched and shared the best email design I could find, 5 days a week. I emailed the best designs to subscribers every week and even daily for some people. It was a labour of love, and would have to be, as any sponsorship or advertising attempts did not bring in any money worth mentioning. But it did pay off when I really needed it.

Unemployed

A few years later I was running a design agency. We did amazing things, won numerous awards but the fun had gone out of it. It was time for a career change and I decided to move from Design to Marketing.

I had a crazy idea, I emailed my subscriber list for BEN and told them I was looking for a job.

The list was about 6,000 subscribers at this stage. I was nervous about opening myself up to the list. My pride was screaming at me not to do it. Like I was belittling myself by begging for a job. The reasonable part of my brain was telling me that this is what marketing is, this is why I built an audience and gave them so much. It was hard to ask but I did. And the BEN audience was wonderful. Within a few days I had five interviews set up for some amazing positions. Three head of marketing and two CEO positions. What's more, I got tons of amazing messages wishing me good luck with the job search and thanks for running BEN. My heart was fit to burst and my confidence was soaring.

Starting a new job is hard. It's all consuming getting up to speed with a new career, a new role, organisation structure and market. Combined with my internal pressure to prove myself as soon as possible and show the trust and belief in me was well placed. As a result of this, I simply had no time and brain space to keep BEN updated. BEN lay idle for about a year and a half. Something I felt very guilty about.

BEN 2 - The return

This month I was able to look at starting up BEN again and I got excited about it.
Last week I started posting a new design each day. On Friday, I needed to restart the email newsletter to subscribers.

Looking at the list I got a shock. In the year and a half since I stopped posting to BEN, the email list grew from 6,000 subscribers to 14,682.

It's probably a post for another time, but the site archive continued to add value while I was gone and people wanted more.

14,682 subscribers. The majority of whom had never actually received an email from me. This needed to be handled delicately. I knew from experience that if I simply restarted the weekly email and sent it on Friday I would get a ton of people marking it as spam, simply because they would not remember subscribing.

On Thursday, I wrote an email to everyone to warn them.
I told them why I was emailing them, reminded them how they signed up but more importantly, I gave them as many ways as possible to unsubscribe. Also, and I feel this is important, I told them my story. I made the email as personal, and personable as possible. Even going so far as to give my personal mobile phone number if anyone had any questions or issues.

People leaving the list is inevitable. Best to direct them to click unsubscribe instead of Spam.

Here is the email I sent.

Beautiful Email Newsletters

```
You can unsubscribe by clicking here.
But first...

Hi John, I know I know, you do not remember me....
At some point you signed up to http://beautiful-email-newsletters.com/ to
get updates about new email design inspiration. Or you downloaded a sample
chapter of my book 30 Days to Sell on the same site  However I started
a new job and made a big career change from design to marketing. This
change involved a learning curve that consumed all my time and I had to
take a break from updating BEN. I apologise for no updates but I hope you
understand.

But we are back! (the royal we, it's still just me). This week I have
resumed posting new, interesting, email designs and will continue this for
the future.

As part of this, every week, subscribers will get an email update with the
best designs of the week and the occasional email marketing tip.

I know you signed up ages ago. And I totally understand if you do not
remember.  So please, if you do not want to get this email unsubscribe
here.
```

Unsubscribe here

```
Still here? Great. Tomorrow (Friday) I will send you the first mail in ages
with new design inspiration.

Thanks for sticking with me,
Alan O'Rourke (alias BEN)


If you have any questions about this mail please email me or give me a ring
on my mobile on NUMBER (Irish time please so I am not asleep :)
```

The results were better than I could have hoped.
Out of 14,682 subscribers, I got 5 people who marked it as spam. 5. I honestly did not imagine it would be so low in my wildest hopes.
1% of the list unsubscribed. 118 people. If they had clicked the spam button the list would be in trouble.
2877 (19.6%) of email addresses bounced which is actually pretty good. Industry benchmarks report that about a third of email addresses become obsolete every year.

And the people had some lovely things to say:

"Welcome back Ben, we have missed you."
"Cheers, Alan! Great to have you back! :)"
"Hi Ben, The fact that you suggested to unsubscribe 4 times in one email is impressive. Nicely done :)"
"haha, loved your email!!! Looking forward to the tomorrow update then!"
"Sounds great 'BEN' Looking forward to seeing what comes through."

On Friday, I sent the first official weekly newsletter in over a year and a half and the response was amazing.
For the next few mails I am going to start every mail with where they subscribed and how to unsubscribe as I know not everyone read the first message.

But for an email I have not send in over a year and a half, I got this reply!

Beautiful Email Newsletters

```
Remember , you can unsubscribe using the link at the
bottom.

If you did not get my mail yesterday, I am Alan from http://beautiful-
email-newsletters.com/ and you previously signed up to get email design
inspiration and/or downloaded a sample of my book 30 Days To Sell. But it
has been AGES! since I last mailed so you might not remember.

If you no longer want this mail or do not remember signing up please
unsubscribe below.

Now on to this weeks design inspiration....
```

"Happy you are back guys! Hooray!"

If you are re-engaging an old list I have these takeaways.

- Expect 1/3 of the list to go dead for every year the list is old.
- Remind people how they subscribed first and give them multiple options to unsubscribe.
- Continue to remind them for the first few weeks. Be personable and honest.
- Remind people they are dealing with a live person.

Finished email marketing plan

So, that's email marketing. If you have been filling out the worksheet as we've gone along, you should now have the basis of an email marketing plan for the future. It should include where to get subscribers, what to email them, how often, and what they can expect to get in return for their effort.

If you have not done so already download the one page worksheet from http://audiencestack.com/static/download-book-1houremail.html and start filling it out.

So, go ahead, fire up an email service like Campaign Monitor or MailChimp, grab one of their ready-made email templates, and send your first email. Above all, enjoy!

Resources and links

A list of email and online marketing resources that I have used and recommend.

Latest email stats and research

- **Email is NOT dead** http://www.emailisnotdead.com/
  Brilliant resource from Mark Brownlow collecting links and numbers of all the latest email market research. You or your boss need convincing to do email marketing? Read this.

Subscriber list building

- **AudienceStack Subscribe Popup Form** http://audiencestack.com
  This is the pop up I use on this site and I love it. Hands down the best tool I have used to build subscribers.

- **Rafflecopter competition widget** https://www.rafflecopter.com/
  A really simple to set up sweepstake widget. Rafflecopter allows multiple ways for a person to enter a competition allowing you to capture their email address, Twitter and Facebook profiles as well as encouraging entrants to share with their own network . I used this to launch the book 30 Days to Sell and the results were great.

- **Email privacy and spam laws around the world (.pdf)**
  http://www.bakermckenzie.com/files/Uploads/Documents/North%20America/DoingBusinessGuide/Houston/bk_globalprivacyhandbook_13.pdf
  This great resource breaks down the privacy and spam laws in every country. Before you hit send, make sure you are covered.

- **The inbox project** http://www.law.cornell.edu/wex/inbox
  A similar research project on the legal and spam laws in different countries.

Email marketing software

- **Campaign Monitor** http://www.campaignmonitor.com/
  I have been using Campaign Monitor for years as my primary email tool. To be honest, most of the email service providers are pretty similar in the features they offer. But I love how easy and fast the Campaign Monitor user interface is.

- **MailChimp** http://mailchimp.com/
  MailChimp is a tool I have had to use a lot for clients. Again the features are pretty complete - it's just a little more fiddly to get to them.

- **Aweber** http://aweber.com/?428910
  When you want to set up an automated sequence of emails when users subscribe or take an action on your website take a look at Aweber. AAweber is the granddaddy of auto-responder emails. The interface is a bit clunky but it is a very powerful tool.

- **Email Vendor Selection** http://www.emailvendorselection.com/email-service-provider-list/
  A pretty complete list of all email service providers and their features.

- **HTML email templates** http://themeforest.net/category/marketing/email-templates?ref=spoiltchild
  Themeforest premium email templates
  Over 550 premium email templates from as little as $8. I have used these often on projects (sometimes just as a basis for my own designs). The time saved not having to worry about coding and testing the emails makes the price an absolute bargain. Responsive email templates are available.

- **Stamplia** http://stamplia.com/
  Less choice than Themeforest but high quality HTML email designs.

Design your own HTML email templates

- **EDM Designer** http://edmdesigner.com/
  A great drag-and-drop email editor to create bulletproof responsive email code.

- **Modern HTML Email: Building Robust, Responsive, & Effective HTML Email** (Book)
  If you want to build responsive HTML email newsletters that display in every screen size? This is the book for you.

- **Ultimate guide to CSS in HTML emails** http://www.campaignmonitor.com/css/
  The only reference you need to know what CSS you can use in your emails. Complete and up to date from the guys at Campaign Monitor.

- **Email testing with Litmus.com** https://litmus.com/
  I have used this service for years and would be in trouble without it. Litmus allows you to upload your finished email newsletter and will show you what it looks like for your readers in all the major email clients such as Outlook, Hotmail, Gmail and even mobile devices. I have been designing emails for years and Litmus still catches issues and saves me from embarrassing mistakes.

- **Responsive email patterns** http://responsiveemailpatterns.com/
  A great collection of patterns or chunks of code you can use to build up your own responsive email newsletter. Brilliant resource.

Inspiration & research

- **Beautiful Email Newsletters** http://beautiful-email-newsletters.com/
- **Really Good Emails** http://reallygoodemails.com/

About the author

Alan describes himself as an ex artist, ex film maker, ex designer, ex product manager and ex entrepreneur. He is currently VP of Growth at OnePageCRM.com and author of a few marketing books. One of which you hold in your hands.

Alan was previously a creative director with over ten years of award winning creative strategy, marketing and user engagement design. Author and speaker, Alan previously ran one of Ireland's leading design agencies where he was nominated for a BAFTA award. Alan later founded online marketing software company Toddle.com, building a user base of almost 30,000 users worldwide before selling the company. He is a graduate of business development in DIT but more importantly studied film and he almost made it to the big time as an extra on TV's A Tale At bedtime with Podge and Rodge playing snooker player #2 but they didn't show his good left side.

 alan@spoiltchild.com

 Linkedin.com/in/spoiltchild

 @alanorourke

You can also follow Alan under the alias @ben_approves as he showcases some of the best email designs on www.beautiful-email-newsletters.com

He writes about sales and marketing at http://audiencestack.com

Marketing Tactics Series

Other books from Alan O'Rourke. http://audiencestack.com/static/books.html

1 hour email marketing
The marketing diploma email course delivered to over 2000 leading companies.

30 days to sell
How the world's leading web sites convert trial users to paying customers.

50 monster ideas to get more website links & customers
Tactics to give your website ranking and traffic a boost.

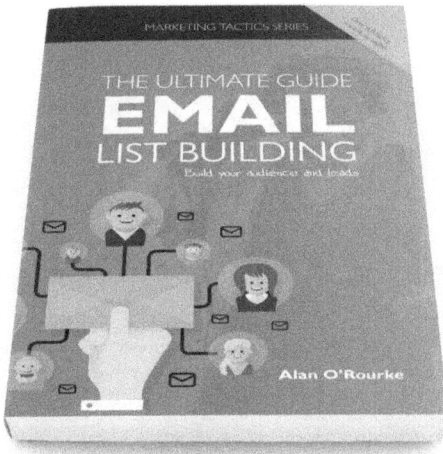

Email list building
Over 200 tactics from leading marketing and sales pros to build your audience and leads.

www.ingramcontent.com/pod-product-compliance
Lightning Source LLC
Chambersburg PA
CBHW061207180526
45170CB00002B/992